Most Haunted CASTLES

YVETTE FIELDING

ILLUSTRATED BY
HANNAH SHAW

Ⓐ

ANDERSEN PRESS

BAMBURGH CASTLE

CODNOR CASTLE

HEVER CASTLE

RUTHIN CASTLE

WHITTINGTON CASTLE

OXFORD CASTLE

TAUNTON CASTLE

PENGERSICK CASTLE

CORVIN CASTLE

HOUSKA CASTLE

INTRODUCTION

My name is Yvette Fielding and I'm a paranormal investigator. Yes, I know that sounds mad. If you'd told me when I was your age that one day I'd be making television shows investigating the paranormal, I'd have said you were crazy. But that is now my life. And I love it.

I began making my TV show *Most Haunted* in 2001, and over the years my fellow investigators and crew on the *Most Haunted* team have come and gone. Now there are only three of us left from the original team: myself, my husband Karl and camera man Stuart. I call the rest of the team 'new' but actually we have been investigating together for nearly ten years. We have a sound and camera crew like most TV shows, as well as investigators who use the equipment needed to explore and record the paranormal. There is friendship, trust and love in our team and I believe that's why we capture such great paranormal activity on camera.

On certain investigations I sometimes invite a demonologist to accompany us. A demonologist is an expert on demons and the dark side of the afterlife. They can deal with negative entities, and wheedle out the shadow demons. I sometimes make contact with very dark souls, like murderers, during my investigations, and to have someone on the team who can cope with those sorts of spirits comes in handy. The strange thing is that as soon as the demonologist calls out and says specific phrases in Latin, weird and frightening things begin to happen. Our sound man, Darren, hates being anywhere near the demonologist. I'm sure it's nothing personal.

I've had the amazing opportunity to investigate paranormal activity in some of the UK's most beautiful castles. Many of them have tragic stories. Their ghosts live within the very fabric of the buildings, in their stones. When I and the *Most Haunted* team arrived at each one, these ghosts loved nothing more than to come out of the darkness and give us all a scare.

As you head with me into these incredible buildings, you'll be introduced to a myriad of strange and frightening spooks: from the spirit of an axe-wielding maiden to the phantom of Vlad the Impaler (that's Dracula, to you and me). These castles hold the memories of life, love, happiness, tragedy, death, murder and sorrow. I hope you enjoy coming with me as we discover all the ghosts that live within these magnificent structures. And after you have finished reading, why not try to visit a castle yourself? But make sure you have your wits about you. You never know who could be watching from the darkness.

PENGERSICK CASTLE

LOCATION

CORNWALL

DATE OF INVESTIGATION

2003

GHOSTS

TWO MONKS

A LITTLE BOY

THE WHITE LADY

JOHN MILITON

MURDERED SAILORS

A DEMON DOG

A LITTLE GIRL

PARANORMAL ACTIVITY

FOOTSTEPS AND CRIES

STRANGE BALLS OF LIGHT

CLOTHING BEING PULLED AND TUGGED

SOUNDS OF A LITTLE GIRL SINGING

APPARITIONS

THE HISTORY

Pengersick Castle

Pengersick Castle is situated on the south coast of Cornwall and was built in the sixteenth century, although the site had been home to the Pengersick family since the twelfth century. Pengersick means 'head of a marshy place' and no wonder, as the stream that runs to the sea contributes to the marshland nearby. Although much of the building has now gone, the castle keep is still intact and dates from 1510.

Henry Pengersick inherited the property at Pengersick from his father Roger in 1329. It's alleged that Henry had a hatred of men of the Church, and that he became violent one night when the local priest, David de Lyspein, and a monk turned up on his doorstep to collect tithes. Henry flew into a terrible rage and violently attacked them. He was excommunicated from the Church for this crime and the villagers steered clear of him, once they knew he was capable of such rages. Henry died in 1343, but his infamous ghost is said to have been seen in and around the property ever since.

The Pengersick family held the estate for

several generations before many of them died in the Black Death in the fourteenth century. The remaining heiress married into a prominent family, who built the present castle in 1510.

During the reign of Henry VIII, the castle was owned by a man called John Militon. It is alleged that he was a murderer who fled justice and hid himself in the remote castle at Pengersick. He improved the castle's defences and he lived there for the rest of his life, never leaving his tower for more than a quick stroll. Rumours about him were rife and it's claimed that he was interested in the Dark Arts and that he used black magic to summon a demon dog. It is also said that he tried to poison his wife's drink, but the cunning lady knew what he was up to and switched the goblets. What truly happened that day, no one knows for sure. But both husband

and wife seem to have survived any attempted poisoning, as records show they died separately some years later.

Another of the castle's legends concerns the treasure of a lost ship, *Santo Antonio*, a Portuguese vessel that went down not far from Pengersick Castle. It's believed a huge amount of wealth was aboard the ship . . . strangely enough, all of it went missing. Allegedly, lepers lured the ship onto the rocks and then made a dash to collect the booty. Some of the shipwrecked sailors tried to escape, but they were then killed at Pengersick Castle. We will never know the truth, but it's rumoured that John Militon used the treasure to restore part of his castle.

THE HAUNTINGS

TWO MONKS

Let's start with the ghost of the monks. There are various accounts of witnesses seeing two monks walking around the grounds. Where have they come from and why are they haunting the location? Some people suggest that Henry Pengersick went so far as to actually murder two men of the Church.

Others have reported seeing just one ghostly monk, and he is described as wearing a typical long habit, but instead of a cowled hood, he's wearing a wide-brimmed hat. This ghost is usually witnessed in the garden, close to the castle and near a stone archway.

A LITTLE BOY

The ghost of a little boy
is reportedly often seen
around the castle. But
he prefers to appear
to women rather than
men. It seems he's an
attention-seeker, because
this little ghost loves
nothing more than to
pull on people's clothes.

THE WHITE LADY

This ghost is said to reside in one of the
bedrooms. She suddenly appears, sitting up in
the bed, clutching her stomach. Could this be
John Militon's long-suffering wife? Did the Dark
Arts fanatic eventually succeed in poisoning her?

JOHN MILITON

If the rumours and legends are true about this man, then his spirit is said to have an energy that isn't seen, but felt. Apparently, his spirit is one of darkness and great evil. As I always say, as in life, so in death. Because he was supposedly involved in the Dark Arts, I wonder if those mystical devilish acts are still being forced upon the castle to this day.

MURDERED SAILORS

In the grounds around the castle, many people have heard the groans and cries of dying men. Emerging out of the fog, sliding across the marshy land, are what appear to be the ghosts of sailors. Many believe that these are the spirits of the sailors who were murdered on that dreadful night when the lepers lured their ship to the shore. It's said some of the sailors escaped and ran up to Pengersick Castle, where they tragically met their end in the grounds of John Militon's home.

A DEMON DOG

There are a few names for the demon dog: padfoot, harbinger of death and Barghest. Many people believe that if you see one, it means that a member of your family will die soon. How pleasant! Other people think they are summoned using the Dark Arts. (Something John Militon apparently was involved in.)

The dog seen at Pengersick is allegedly huge in size and has eyes like red flaming coals.

A LITTLE GIRL

Who the ghost of this little girl is, no one knows. But whoever she is, she's not very pleasant. Eyewitnesses report hearing her singing. They follow the sound up to the top of the keep and, there on the roof, she can be seen dancing and twirling around, enticing the viewer to follow her. It's believed that unsuspecting people have sometimes followed her, only to topple over the wall to their deaths.

THE INVESTIGATION

I remember very clearly arriving at Pengersick Castle. It was a cold, damp day and as the car pulled up the drive, a tall, dark tower rose up in front of us. As I looked at the building where I and the *Most Haunted* team were to spend the night, my skin began to crawl. Something wasn't right. I felt as though I was being watched. None of us were looking forward to this investigation.

Our minds were soon distracted, though, as we began to film outside in the grounds. And we had some fun trying to put up two tents. My idea was that some members of the team would spend the night outside: two female members of my team in one tent, and in the other, two rather nervous young men. Seeing as there were reports of ghostly sailors, monks and a demon dog appearing in the grounds, it made sense that some of them should draw the short straw and sleep outside.

As the night drew in and the temperature dropped, we began to gather our ghost-hunting equipment together and split up into groups. Armed with our night-vision cameras, temperature guns and electromagnetic field meters, we began the investigation.

I had decided to start my evening in the castle keep itself, in one particular room called the 'solar'. An ancient winding stone staircase took me and two other members of my team up and up into the room. It certainly didn't feel sunny as I sat there in the dark, huddled inside my coat to stop myself shaking from the cold.

I panned my night-vision camera around the dark room, waiting anxiously for something to

happen. And it wasn't long before it did. Suddenly I caught sight of a lovely silver orb floating right across the doorway. I called out to the others about what I'd seen but before they could reply, an enormous bang ricocheted around the room. We all jumped out of our skins.

'What the hell was that?' I yelled, running towards where the sound had come from.

'I think it was the door downstairs,' said one of my companions.

We quickly moved out of the room and down the stone steps to find an open door leading outside.

'But that was closed before,' I whispered.

Another member of my team agreed.

We opened and shut the door, to see if that was the noise we'd heard. It certainly sounded like it.

I was excited because it wasn't a windy night, there wasn't even a breeze. What could have lifted up the heavy metal latch and opened the door, made it bang hard and then opened it again? We didn't know, but we all agreed that the atmosphere around us had changed. It was as if a black cloud had come into our space and was trying to smother us.

We waited in vain, hoping for something else to happen. I called out: 'Who's here with us?' into the silence, and held my breath for as long as I could . . . but nothing.

Meanwhile, outside, the two groups couldn't believe what they had managed to film on their cameras. Although nothing could actually be seen, apart from their terrified faces, it was the noises they had captured that were fascinating! Many of the sounds could, of course, be put down to small animals rustling about in the undergrowth. But some of them were definitely loud, heavy footsteps, breaking twigs and branches as they stomped around the tents. Yet when they felt brave enough, the ghost hunters opened the tent flaps to find no one, absolutely no one there.

After exploring inside the keep, I decided to move to a different part of the castle. I was intrigued by the battlements, where the ghost of a little girl is said to lure people to their deaths with her singing and dancing.

Would she try to lure me up there? I hoped to hear her singing, although I admit I was terrified as I made the long climb up the winding stone staircase again. As I got to the top and walked out onto the roof, I was disappointed not to hear or see anything. I stood and called out, but I still heard nothing.

The same couldn't be said for poor Karl and his fellow investigator, though. Both men were walking down the gravel path towards the main entrance of the castle keep when, all of a sudden, they quite clearly heard loud footsteps running up behind them. Karl screamed.

The pair were so scared, they ran to the car and locked themselves inside. But even then, you can clearly hear footsteps walking close to the vehicle on the camera footage.

So, what had they and the rest of the team witnessed outside? Certainly not woodland animals, that's for sure. I wonder if it could be the spirits of the monks, trying to escape the violent Henry Pengersick.

And what about the slamming door, and the negative energy that I and my team members experienced in the solar? Was that the ghost of evil John Militon, perhaps?

After that night, some members of the crew weren't too keen to come on another investigation. One of them said those footsteps had really unnerved him and he needed a break from ghost hunting for a while.

Pengersick is allegedly one of the most haunted castles in the UK, but even though I and other members of my team did experience things there that no one can explain, I couldn't help but feel a little disappointed that I hadn't *seen* anything. Being a ghost hunter, I always want more.

? DID YOU KNOW? ?

The sighting of a devil dog at Peel Castle on the Isle of Man allegedly caused the death of a man. One night a drunk guard at the castle bravely walked down a dark passage to confront a large, four-legged beast. Upon his return, his fellow guards could see how shocked and terrified he was. He never recovered. The poor man died three days later. After the brave guard's sad and unexpected demise, his colleagues sealed up the passageway so no one would ever have to come face to face with the devilish hound again.

RUTHIN CASTLE

LOCATION
NORTH WALES

DATE OF FIRST INVESTIGATION
2018

GHOSTS
THE GREY LADY

THE ONE-GLOVED SOLDIER

A LITTLE GIRL

THE WHITE LADY

PARANORMAL ACTIVITY
KNOCKING

MOVING OBJECTS

FOOTSTEPS

SINGING AND WHISTLING

AN EVIL ENTITY

POLTERGEIST ACTIVITY

THE HISTORY

Ruthin Castle

The first documented fortification on this site was created in 1277 by the Welsh prince, Dafydd ap Gruffydd. He had been gifted the land by Edward I of England in gratitude for his assistance in the invasion of North Wales. The castle was a strategic stronghold in the eventual defeat of the Welsh by the English in 1282.

Soon after, the de Grey family took over the castle and it remained in their hands until 1508 when it was sold to Henry VII and passed down to Henry VIII. When Charles I inherited it in the seventeenth century he sold the castle and grounds, which were in disrepair, to raise some much-needed funds.

During the Civil War, the castle was quickly repaired at the Crown's expense and used to house Royalist soldiers. In 1646, Ruthin Castle underwent an eleven-week siege by the Parliamentarians, who heavily attacked the walls with artillery. The Royalists eventually surrendered and the castle walls were torn down in 1648 and used to build many local houses.

Nearly two centuries later, the castle was bought by a wealthy family who set about building a new mansion within the old castle walls. The work was completed in 1879 and many aristocratic and royal guests were entertained there – including the Prince of Wales (later King Edward VII), who had an affair with the owner's wife.

In 1923, the castle was turned into a private clinic but was sold during the 1950s. In the early 1960s it was bought again and turned into a hotel, which it remains to this day. King Charles III stayed there on his way to his investiture as the Prince of Wales back in 1969.

The castle has many ghost stories, and numerous strange paranormal occurrences have been reported over the years, but the most famous ghost is that of the Grey Lady.

THE HAUNTINGS

THE GREY LADY

It is said the Grey Lady was the wife of the second-in-command of the castle. She discovered that her powerful husband was having an affair with a local woman. In a jealous rage, she murdered her husband's lover with an axe. Legend has it, she buried her victim's body parts all over the castle grounds – although to date, no human remains have ever been found.

When caught, it is believed the Grey Lady went mad. She was tried for her crimes and executed. She was not allowed to be buried within the grounds of the castle and it's said that her ghost rampages around the building in a fury, wielding her axe and terrorising anyone who dares to get in her way.

THE ONE-GLOVED SOLDIER

This spectre has been seen walking around the castle in different areas. It's believed he was a loyal soldier to King Edward I and, along with many others, died in a battle trying to defend his master's fortress.

Most people who are lucky enough to see him report that he only seems to be wearing one glove. How curious. I wonder what this could mean. Perhaps he was an archer? Witnesses report that this apparition doesn't interact or look at any of the unsuspecting guests; he seems to be on his way to do something important.

A LITTLE GIRL

The ghost of a mischievous little girl has often been seen running up and down the corridors and halls inside the castle. Lots of hotel guests have heard the sound of running feet and a little girl singing and giggling. They then report hearing a *knock, knock, knock* at their room door, but when they go to answer it, no one is there.

THE WHITE LADY

This ghost has been witnessed on several occasions, but only in the banqueting hall. Some people see her standing on the minstrels' gallery, dressed all in white, whilst others see her floating around the main hall.

THE INVESTIGATION

I was keen to get on with the investigation as soon as the sun went down. I had heard that one area in particular seemed to be a hotspot for paranormal activity, so I wanted to go there first.

Down one of the many long corridors in the hotel is Room 222. It's here that many overnight guests have reported hearing knocking on the door, only to find no one there. Could this be our chance to glimpse the ghost of the little girl so many visitors have seen and heard?

Guests have also been woken by the sounds of furniture being dragged around on the floor above them, accompanied by heavy footsteps. The creepy thing about Room 222 is that just inside the main door, there is a door off to the left.

It's always kept locked but when you do open it, you find a flight of deteriorating stairs leading up to an old abandoned apartment. Who lived up there? No one knows for sure, but whoever did doesn't seem to want to leave. This apartment sits directly above Room 222 and is where the night-time noises reportedly come from.

On the night of the investigation, I walked down the long corridor to Room 222, the light from my torch bouncing off the floor. I wasn't alone – I'm not that daft! I took my husband Karl and our resident sceptic, Glen Hunt, with me.

I had sent my other investigators off into various other locations around the castle. Two of the camera men, Gregg and Stuart, were to head to a room just off the banqueting hall next to the minstrels' gallery upstairs. And the demonologist was taking his chances in the cellar – which was once the morgue when the castle was a clinic.

As soon as I walked in through the door to Room 222, I felt quite dizzy. The sensation became worse when Karl led me and Glen up to the apartment above. I actually thought I was going to faint on the grimy staircase. What was happening to me? Suddenly, deep, heavy knocking and tapping began to pound around us.

I called out: 'Do you mean us harm? If you do, knock twice for yes, once for no.'

Two loud thuds came from the floorboards. I gulped and looked around at my companions. Were they as nervous as me? I suspected that Karl was – but Glen? He always tries to think of the logical explanation for these strange occurrences, and that's how it should be. But when I looked at his face, all I could see in the torchlight was a look of total and utter bewilderment.

Back down in the cellar, the demonologist was calling out too. He walked slowly around the pitch-black stone room, trying to steady his camera as he talked to a spirit that allegedly causes chaos and terror whenever staff enter. In fact, some of them refuse to go into the cellar because they believe that something evil lurks within it.

At first, the demonologist shouted out in Latin, hoping that the ancient language would pull the spirit out of the shadows, and it did.

'Hello, who's there?' he said, pointing the camera towards something he had just seen. He felt someone walk up close to him, and then the camera just cut out, losing all power . . .

Meanwhile, my two other investigators, Gregg and Stuart, were making their way up the stairs to a little dressing room next to the minstrels' gallery. On the way up, Stuart showed the EMF meter to the camera. It was fluctuating. The lights were moving rapidly from the lower end of the scale, right up to the top: a great sign that a spirit was nearby.

As they made their way into the little dressing room, the EMF meter was still flashing, and when they stood quietly in the dark, they realised that the room was getting colder and colder. They placed their torch beams in front of their mouths and breathed out. Later, when we watched the camera footage, we could see their icy breath swirling about their faces. Something was definitely with them, but who or what it was, they couldn't say.

Back in the apartment above Room 222, the knocking had become louder and louder, until it found the rhythm of a heartbeat. I had experienced this on other investigations. I often wonder if it's the spirit trying to tell me that they are alive. Although we cannot see them, they create an invisible energy that is still around us.

Glen looked around on the floor and traced the sound to a huge gap in the floorboards. Yet within that gap there was nothing but air.

I began to feel ill again and had to kneel down. I had the sensation of a huge heavy weight pressing down on my head and shoulders. I suspected that this entity, whoever it was, was coming too close to me and this was why I was feeling ill. Just to confirm it, I asked the spirit to knock if indeed it was affecting me. Two enormous knocks pounded under our feet.

Glen suddenly asked Karl if there was anyone standing behind him. Karl positioned the camera and focussed in just over Glen's shoulder but couldn't see anything. Glen said that he really felt as though someone were standing behind him. Just then, the sound of heavy footsteps could be heard walking all around us.

'Were you standing behind me?' Glen called out, and to his amazement there were two knocks.

We had been in this apartment now for over an hour and I was wondering how the others were getting on, particularly the demonologist, who was on his own in the cellar. We all had our phones and no one had rung for help, but Karl volunteered to go and check anyway. He could see that I was worried. So off he went, leaving me and Glen alone in the dark.

My heart was banging violently in my chest and suddenly I felt deep breathing really close to me. I jumped and caused poor Glen to cry out in fright.

'I heard breathing,' I whimpered.

'Are you sure it wasn't me?'

'Let's hold our breath and see if we can both hear it,' I suggested.

So we held our breath. Terrifyingly, we could both hear a man breathing really close beside us in the dark.

We'd had enough. We made our way to the stairs, where immediately Glen announced that he was feeling lightheaded and very hot.

I wasn't taking any chances, I needed to get Glen out of there before he collapsed. But just as we were making our way down the stairs, Karl shouted up: 'Yvette, Glen, the demonologist's unconscious in the cellar, we need a paramedic.'

Well, we ran as fast as we could to the cellar, and there we found the demonologist lying face down on an old sofa. After calling his name and getting no response, Gregg, who was also our first aider, managed to get him to come round.

Paramedics were called and after check-ups, the demonologist was given the all clear. We asked him what had happened down there.

'I don't know, but something bad is in that cellar, and I don't want to go back in there again.'

When a demonologist says something like that, you'd think I'd stay out the cellar. Think again! I felt I had to go in and find out what had affected him. And so I took Karl and Stuart with me into the bowels of the castle, and asked Glen and Gregg to go to Room 222 to set up the EVP machine.

I love electronic voice phenomena. This is where spirits use sound waves to communicate with us. It's like using a telephone, but in our case we use a computer. I like to place a laptop in a haunted room and leave it recording in the hopes that a ghost will talk and give us a message. Over the years we've managed to capture some fantastic ghostly voices. Hopefully we would catch some spirit audibles in Room 222 . . .

Walking down the steep stone steps into the cellar, I was faced with lots of old furniture and boxes, all stacked on top of each other. There were a few small tunnels leading off, and a couple of larger vaults, one of which was where we had found the demonologist.

It was so cold down there, my teeth chattered as I stood in the total darkness. I called out, 'Who's here with us? Make yourself known.'

Suddenly something hit the floor, as if it had been thrown at us. But when we searched around, we couldn't find anything.

Then we all heard a rustling noise, as if someone were moving around the stacked-up boxes. We went to where the noise had come from, but again we found nothing.

Without any warning, something heavy fell behind me. It made an enormous thud and I screamed. I hadn't moved or touched anything; when we shone the torch on the object that had fallen, we discovered a huge wooden pillar on the floor.

Something had moved it.

'Come out of the shadows, show yourself to us!' I shouted angrily.

Karl gasped and jumped suddenly as he pointed to a dark archway where he was sure he had just seen a black shadow moving.

The breathing was back, this time louder and more aggressive, almost like growls. We hoped we had caught the sound on camera and decided that enough was enough.

As we were leaving, I called out one last time, asking the ghost to show itself.

Suddenly, looming large at the back of the cellar, was a man's white face. He was terrifying. I'm sure this ghost was the one responsible for hurting the demonologist, and I believe he is still there to this day. I don't think we will ever know his identity. Maybe he prefers it that way.

DID YOU KNOW?

Demons were originally angels. According to Christian scripture, Lucifer, otherwise known as Satan, was one of God's favourite angels. But Lucifer became a little too confident and rebellious and so God cast him, and two hundred of his treacherous friends, out of Heaven, where they all fell into the fiery tongues of Hell.

CODNOR CASTLE

DATE OF INVESTIGATION
2016

LOCATION
DERBYSHIRE

THE GHOSTS
A POLTERGEIST

SOME CHILDREN

A MURDERER

THE HANGED MAN

A BLACK SHADOW

PARANORMAL ACTIVITY
DARK SHADOWS

OBJECTS MOVED AND THROWN

SCREAMS, GROWLS, CHILDREN'S LAUGHTER AND SINGING

SMELLS OF PERFUME AND SMOKE

THE HISTORY

Codnor Castle

This now-ruined castle stands overlooking the Erewash Valley in Derbyshire and dates back as far as the eleventh century when William the Conqueror gave the land it stands on to one of his Norman knights.

By 1211, an incredibly powerful family lived

in the castle – the de Greys (yes, distant relations of the family who were living in Ruthin Castle). Henry de Grey, the patriarch of the family, who was a favourite in the court of King John, oversaw the castle's twenty-year construction. He loved its location because it was close to Sherwood Forest. In fact, many of the law men of the time stayed at the castle, and the building was also used as a court where people would be tried and judged before the guilty were taken to Nottingham Castle for execution.

Eventually the de Grey family line died out, and the castle passed through various owners, including Henry VII, until it was sold to an archbishop in 1632. But the archbishop did not want to live there, so he split the estate into tenanted farms and moved away, leaving the castle empty. Soon the locals began to take the castle's stone to build homes nearby. The largest one, named Castle Farm House, was built alongside the ruins in the 1640s.

As time went by, the castle fell deeper into disrepair. Various minerals were eventually discovered under the castle and on the land, and so foundry furnaces were built nearby.

In the nineteenth century, the castle and its land were purchased by the Butterley Company, a business that mined ironstone. In the 1960s, a UK coal mining company took control.

The castle is now run by the Codnor Castle Heritage Trust, which aims to preserve what's left of the magnificent structure. The ruins are sensational to look at, and it's been said that the ghost of a man wearing a black cloak can be seen wandering in its shadows.

But it's Castle Farm House that really intrigued

me and my team. Apparently, no one has been able to live in the building since the 1970s, as there are just too many ghosts for the tenants to cope with.

I needed to find out more and so decided to spend a night with my team in the shadow of the ruins and see if we could last twenty-four hours inside Castle Farm House. Which, by the way, now has a nickname amongst the locals: Hell House!

THE HAUNTINGS

A POLTERGEIST

It is said that there is a poltergeist haunting Castle Farm House and no one has been able to live there for half a century. This noisy ghost, whoever they are, certainly likes to make their presence known. All sorts of objects have been thrown through the air – from a beautiful jewelled necklace to heavy metal beds. No wonder people are too scared to stay.

SOME CHILDREN

The ghosts of children have been heard many times in the farm house's attic – giggling, running and singing. The ghosts have rarely been seen though, so no one knows which time period they're from.

A MURDERER

It's alleged that a man killed his daughter in the farm house during the 1970s. A dark and evil presence is often felt around the house and many people can't stand the feeling that comes over them if they stay too long. They also complain of headaches and sickness and as if they're being closely watched.

Could the spirit of the murderer still be present in the cottage? And if so, what harm could he possibly do to the living? We were about to find out.

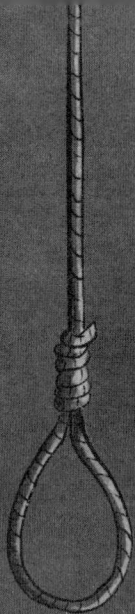

THE HANGED MAN

Apparently, during the 1950s, one of the past owners hanged himself from the attic window. It's believed that his sad ghost still resides here, and some believe he's protecting visitors from something evil that lurks within the house.

A BLACK SHADOW

This elusive ghost has been seen flitting in and around the castle ruins for many years, but no one is sure who this spirit is. Maybe it could be one of the many family members that lived in the castle or perhaps it is a servant or guardsman.

THE INVESTIGATION

I was fascinated by this location. Allegedly there had been suicides and murders committed here. But why? What was it about this place which spurred so many catastrophes? Hopefully I would get some answers during our night here.

When we arrived, the first thing I insisted upon was placing a few night-vision cameras around the castle ruins – just in case we happened to capture the famous shadowy, ghostly figure. The identity of this spectre has never been uncovered. Whoever the ghost was, I hoped we could capture it on film. Once that was done and I was satisfied we had all the angles covered, we took a short stroll over to the haunted farm house.

As soon as I stepped over the threshold on that dark winter's day, I shuddered. Not from the cold but from the negative feeling that consumed me. Something wasn't right here at all, and I knew that we had to be careful.

As I walked around, the house just looked like any other farm house. The rooms were an average size and an old staircase twisted around within, like an old man's backbone trying to support the rest of its heavy load.

On the top floor was what looked like a cupboard, but when it was opened it revealed another set of stairs leading to the attic. I only peeked inside but I immediately got a feeling of dread. Other members of the *Most Haunted* team felt the same way.

On the other hand, Glen Hunt, our team sceptic, was convinced we were only feeling discombobulated because of the stories we had been told about the castle and the farm house.

'If you hadn't been told about the history, would you still feel the same?' he asked us.

It was a good point, but we all insisted that something didn't feel right and we sensed we were being watched.

For this particular investigation I wanted to do a trigger object experiment. This is where an object is used to entice the spirit to interact with us – either by moving the object or making it disappear completely.

Recently, Karl and I had been given the delightful present of an old doll. Allegedly it was haunted, although I was a little doubtful

of that. I had never had any experiences with haunted objects before. Still, I decided to give the doll the benefit of the doubt and brought it along to the investigation.

I reckoned that the best place to put the doll would be in the attic, as this was where the voices of children had been heard. Would the children come out to play with the doll? I hoped so. I got my team to stand the doll in front of a wooden roof support and set up a camera to record it all the time we were in the building.

Then we began to film. For *Most Haunted*, I always start off by walking around the different haunted areas, explaining what paranormal activity has occurred in each of the spaces. When I got up to the attic and began to speak to the camera, something was suddenly hurled at me. I screamed and the rest of the crew began to look around to see what had been thrown.

When I found the object, the breath left my body. A black crucifix lay on the dusty ground. I know it wasn't there before. It's something that we definitely would have noticed.

Seeing the cross really shook us all. Where had it come from? And what did it mean? I wondered if it could be from the ghost of the man who had committed suicide. Maybe he was trying to protect us. But from what?

Now we were all on our guard. Even Glen.

I called out for the spirit who had thrown the object to communicate with us by knocking and tapping.

'Did you mean to harm us?' I whispered.

One loud bang came back – which meant 'No'.

I asked another question: 'Are we safe?' A bang emanated around the attic. Just the one, though. This wasn't good at all.

After we had filmed the introduction pieces to the show, it was the time where I got to say the immortal words, 'Let's turn all the lights off . . .' Normally I would be very excited at this point, but in that farm house I was just full of dread.

I felt it was right that the whole team stayed together to begin with, until we had gained a little confidence and got to know the building better. So we all went into one of the bedrooms. Icy cold blasts of air rolled around the pitch-black room and Darren, our sound recordist, suddenly complained that he couldn't catch his breath.

In a flash, Karl swung round to look behind him. He'd just heard a child's laugh, he said.

We all moved into the adjoining room where Karl thought the laughter had come from. It was a small space and could only just accommodate us all.

Darren insisted that he could smell a strong floral perfume, and then knocking began to boom through the walls.

As soon as I asked for the knocking to be made louder, it stopped completely.

Normally when you're dealing with a benevolent, kindly spirit, they will do anything they can to enhance communication with the living. But when they suddenly stop, it often suggests that the spirit you're talking to isn't very pleasant – or likes being mischievous.

I ushered the team out onto the stairwell and we all heard the sound of footsteps coming up the stairs towards us. Loud and heavy.

'I have a bad feeling about this,' said the demonologist.

Now, when a demonologist says they have a bad feeling about something, this doesn't bode well. In about 90% of the investigations where he has uttered these words, something awful has happened.

I called out: 'Who's here with us?' A response came in the rustling of clothes, again on the stairs.

'Whoever you are, do something to get rid of us.'

Bizarrely enough, in that moment, we all smelled smoke. It wasn't tobacco smoke, it was fire. The smell dissipated as quickly as it had come but it was definitely there, we had all experienced it.

Now was the time to split the team up. But as I began to pair up team members, we all heard a man's loud groan. It was caught by our sound equipment, and even to this day when I hear it, it sends chills down my spine.

Karl then stumbled back and pointed at an open doorway behind us all.

'There's a man!' he shouted. 'He's standing just there.'

As we all ran to where the shadowy figure had been seen, the temperature in that area began to drop rapidly.

'Do you want us to go up into the attic?' I called out to the spirit.

Two knocks came straight back, meaning 'Yes'.

Nervously, we all agreed to go up the small staircase which led to the attic. As soon as we walked into the room, the demonologist said,

'The hairs are all standing up on the back of my neck.'

Unexpectedly, we then heard a peculiar noise. It sounded like metal hitting the floor. We quickly turned on our torches to discover lots of old pennies lying around our feet. We closely inspected them and found that they all dated from the late 1800s up to the 1940s. We were astounded.

What on earth was happening and why?

It seemed that every time I said, 'It's time for us to split up,' something weird happened. It was almost as if someone or something didn't want us to go our separate ways. Was a spirit really trying to protect us? It seemed that way. But what was it trying to protect us from?

The clinking noise happened once more: more pennies clattering to the floor. Glen's face was a picture as he pointed at the ceiling and gasped, 'I saw them all fall from the ceiling!'

That was a sweet moment for me. The fact that a sceptic had witnessed something paranormal and couldn't explain it was wonderful. Surely he had to believe now!

At this point, we did manage to split up into smaller groups. I stayed in the attic with Darren and Gregg, the camera operator. With all the others gone, we felt more vulnerable and pretty scared.

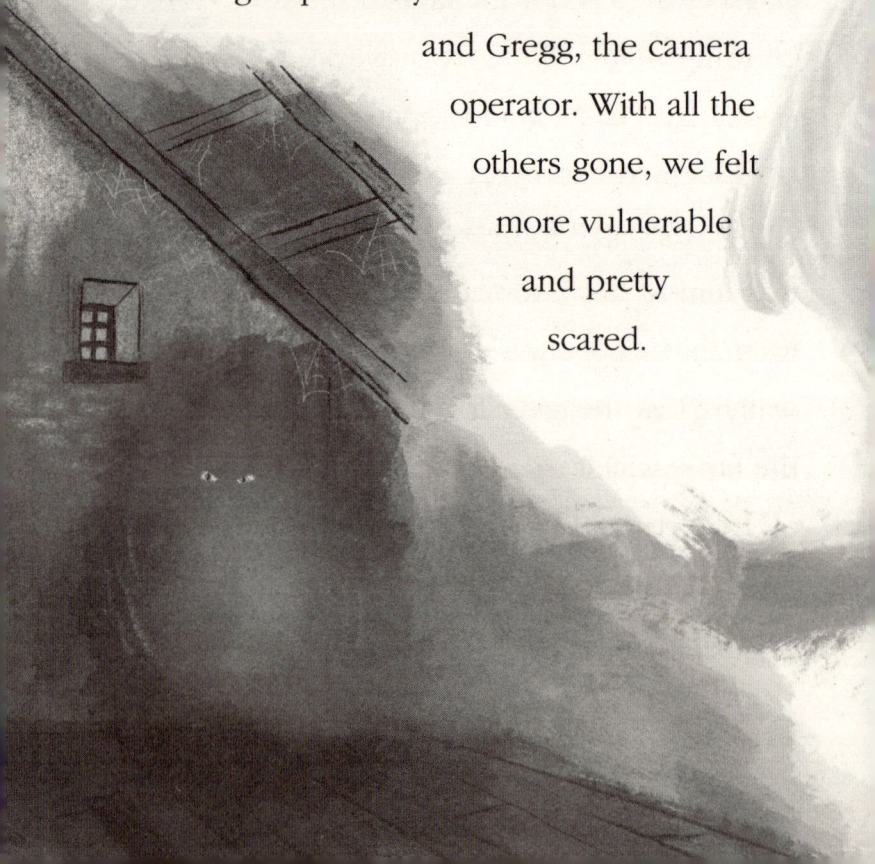

Suddenly, Darren said he'd seen a pair of eyes watching us from the other end of the attic. He was terrified and grabbed my arm for support. I tried to rationalise the situation, reminding him that whoever had given us the coins was probably a good spirit and hopefully protecting us. I secretly hoped I was right.

As Gregg trained the camera to where Darren had reported seeing two eyes, he suddenly exclaimed that he could see a grey mist emerging and that it was coming towards us. Well, as you can imagine, we were frightened, but at the same time pretty excited. Could this be a ghost trying to manifest? We all stood completely still and watched as the grey fog moved and twisted in the far reaches of the attic. What the hell was it?

I called out to it, and Darren put his hand out and stepped forward gingerly. Suddenly he snatched it back and said that the mist had twisted in between all his fingers. He seemed really emotional and pretty mesmerised by what he'd just experienced.

Just then, the rest of the team came back up the stairs to join us and it wasn't long before we were picking up anomalies on the soundtrack: a loud whistle and a growl.

Karl and the demonologist weren't convinced by my theory that this was a good spirit trying to protect us. They thought something evil was present and playing with us.

I stood close to where Darren had seen the eyes peering out, and immediately I felt very emotional and began to cry. I sensed that something terrible had happened in that room and I also felt quite strongly that it had something to do with a child. A girl.

I explained to the others what I was feeling. I've never claimed to be a psychic but sometimes we are all capable of picking up on feelings and atmospheres and I don't think people should ignore those signs.

'Did something horrible happen in this room?' I asked, hoping to get a response with knocking.

Two knocks, meaning 'Yes'.

'Was someone murdered in here?'

Again, two knocks answered my question.

The demonologist then told me that he'd been digging into the history of the farm house and that yes, it was rumoured that a young girl had been killed there. But where, he did not know.

'Was a girl murdered in this room?' I asked the spirit.

Two knocks came back quickly, and I believed them.

I decided to leave Stuart and the demonologist upstairs in the attic, whilst I and other members of the team went to investigate the rest of the house.

Once alone, the demonologist called out for any demons to stay with him rather than follow me. And, bizarre as this sounds, his chants and strange Latin words did seem to have a weird effect. More coins rained down from the ceiling, but this time they were seemingly thrown with violence, one hitting Stuart hard in the back.

Then a very loud crash splintered through the air. Stuart ran to where the noise was coming from and discovered a steel bed in the middle of the floor. We had all seen the bed butted up against the wall previously. But now here it was, right in the centre.

As the demonologist and Stuart were discussing what had just happened, they suddenly smelled smoke. Turning round, they could see black billowing fumes coming from where the doll had been placed. Stuart ran over and there, standing in a bright orange and black haze, was the doll, beginning to melt as angry hot flames licked at its sweet angelic face.

Lots of screaming and pandemonium ensued as the rest of us were told through the walkie-talkies to get out of the building because there was a fire. Everyone scrambled out but once the fire had been put out, we all went back into the attic to see exactly what had happened.

To this day, I'll never understand it. Why did the doll spontaneously combust? I decided to stop the investigation then and there. This had gone too far, and I wasn't about to let any of my team get hurt.

We put the doll back into a wooden box and brought it home to Cheshire. I can't tell you how worried I was sitting in the car, knowing that the haunted doll was in the boot. I felt very uneasy all the way home. As soon as it was possible, we sent it to the Cheshire Fire and Rescue Service for analysis. The result came back that no accelerants had been used and that it was a complete mystery as to how the doll had caught fire.

Sometime later we did go back to the castle and the farm house, and once more placed cameras around the ruins. Sadly, as before, nothing paranormal was captured in the ruins.

The dark shadowy spectre had eluded our cameras – but something awful was experienced yet again. This time, by Karl. His arm was set ablaze! Thankfully he wasn't alone; he was with Stuart, and they got his coat off and stamped the fire out. But Karl's arm was burned. Again, the coat was analysed by the fire service, and the same results as before came back.

After this final incident, it was enough for us to stay away. This time for good.

DID YOU KNOW?

Human spontaneous combustion is a phenomenon that, to this day, has confounded scientists and doctors alike. There have been many cases throughout the world where objects and humans have literally gone up in flames for no apparent reason.

One such case, and possibly the most famous, is that of Countess Cornelia Bandi. In 1731, her unusual death caught the attention of the world. Her charred remains were discovered at the bottom of her bed but none of the bedclothes had been burned nor the rest of the contents in the room. The world-famous author Charles Dickens was a true believer in spontaneous human combustion and was so enraptured by this case, he used it in one of his books, *Bleak House*, to kill off one of his characters.

BAMBURGH CASTLE

DATE OF INVESTIGATION

2006

LOCATION

NORTHUMBERLAND

GHOSTS

THE PINK LADY

SECOND WORLD WAR
BRITISH SOLDIER

DOCTOR JOHN SHARP

GREEN JANE

PARANORMAL ACTIVITY

COLD SPOTS

SOUNDS OF A PIANO
PLAYING

GHOSTLY HANDS
CLUTCHING AT GUESTS

FEELINGS OF HYSTERIA
AND SICKNESS

SOUNDS OF A BABY
CRYING

SOUNDS OF CHILDREN
RUNNING

THE HISTORY

Bamburgh Castle

This stunning and imposing ancient structure sits proudly high above the stormy waters of the North Sea. It's an enormous site that originally housed a far smaller timber construction built around AD 547 by Ida the Flame Bearer, an Anglo-Saxon king.

It was because of its fantastic strategic position, right in the middle of the lands and kingdoms to the north and south, that many landowners and monarchs wanted this place for themselves. Whoever owned the castle would be a very powerful person indeed. In fact, the fortress was the seat of the kings of Northumbria for many years. Bamburgh has witnessed many battles, sieges and murders during the attempts to grasp this powerful stronghold.

During the infamous Viking raids, the castle was pillaged and some of the buildings inside the fortress were burned. It was later rebuilt by the Normans and became the property of the English monarchy until the mid-sixteenth century.

During the eighteenth century, Doctor John Sharp was the first person to fully restore the castle, adding many extensions, ramparts and even cannons.

Within its lifetime, Bamburgh Castle has been a school, a military headquarters, an infirmary and a convalescent home for injured soldiers during the Second World War.

So, with all this history, it's no wonder that this amazing structure is reported to be very haunted, and I and the rest of my investigative team couldn't wait to spend the night there.

THE HAUNTINGS

THE PINK LADY

A sad love story surrounds the haunting by this Northumbrian princess. A beautiful young woman had fallen head over heels in love with a boy. Her father was most displeased with the match and made the decision to send the boy away for seven years overseas. Her father believed that, over time, his daughter's affections for the unsuitable boy would dampen. But he was wrong. The young broken-hearted princess fell into a deep depression. What could her father do? He decided to tell his daughter that her love had married another. He thought this news would definitely bring her to her senses. To help her try to forget her heartbreak, the king ordered a beautiful pink dress to be made for the princess, believing that this would finally bring her out of her misery.

Yet the young princess put on the dress and took herself up to the battlements, where she threw herself off, plunging to her death on the jagged rocks below.

Apparently, her beautiful apparition is seen floating through the corridors, wearing her pretty pink gown, every seven years. She has also been seen moving silently down the path and onto the beach, where it is said she looks out, hoping to see her true love finally return.

SECOND WORLD WAR BRITISH SOLDIER

During the Second World War, the castle was used as a convalescent home. It's said that a young male patient shot himself there and tragically died. His ghost has been seen sitting at the bottom of some stairs at the end of a long corridor.

Cold spots are also felt in this area, and many tell the tale of a small icy hand trying to hold theirs. All these paranormal phenomena happen in what's called the Tapestry Corridor.

DOCTOR JOHN SHARP

This hugely important figure associated with the castle and its rebuild has been seen regularly by visitors and residents.

People often witness a misty figure walking around all areas of the castle and it's only when they see his portrait that they recognise who it is they have just seen. It's believed that Doctor John Sharp was so in love with Bamburgh that he absolutely refuses to leave.

GREEN JANE

This ghost has been witnessed walking slowly near the clock tower. She is carrying a bundle under an emerald green cloak. The sad story goes that one night a starving woman holding a baby in her arms tried desperately to gain entrance to the castle. She wanted shelter, and of course, food for her and her baby. But the guards decided to jeer at her and push her away. In doing so, it's believed that the poor woman fell, and that she and her baby tumbled down the steep stone steps to their deaths.

Since her terrible demise her ghost has been seen near the clock tower, falling and crying out for help. People have actually rushed to help her and the baby, but when they get close, the ghostly vision just fades away.

THE INVESTIGATION

I'll never forget the day I saw Bamburgh for the first time. It was a cold and blustery afternoon; the sky was grey, and the sea looked angry. As we drove towards the mammoth structure, my jaw hit the floor. The huge, stunning castle seemed to have grown out of the ground, its stone blending in perfectly with its rugged surroundings.

It felt like we had gone back in time and I half-expected to see a stampede of snorting horses complete with sword-wielding warriors on their backs come galloping up to us. What a place to visit! What a place to live in! I couldn't wait to get inside.

There were great halls and corridors and fabulous rooms within the castle, one after the other. Where to start the investigation? I knew as soon as I walked into the Tapestry Corridor, and suddenly felt very cold, that this was the place to begin.

We had set up various cameras and gathered baseline readings of the rooms we were to investigate. This involved taking the average temperature and air pressure, sweeping the room for electromagnetic fields, and finding out where the electrical power sources were. We also took note of any creaky floorboards, loose window frames and noisy water pipes. All this information would be used as a reference if anything paranormal were to occur. So, if a growl is heard and picked up on the footage, we can look at the baseline test and see if anything natural within the room could have caused the noise. If not, then it could very well be paranormal.

As usual, when darkness fell, the property took on a completely different atmosphere. I was no longer gazing at the beautiful portraits of long-dead lords, ladies and kings. Now I was staring down long dark corridors, not really sure what I was looking at. Was that a statue or a person standing there?

The *Most Haunted* team and I went into the Tapestry Corridor. This was the area in which I had felt a chill earlier. I felt there was a presence here, but would it come out to play?

Sitting at a table near the stairs where the ghost of a young Second World War soldier had been seen, I called out into the dark and asked whether he was with us, hoping that the presence would respond.

Instantly the table banged up and down heavily. Everyone jumped, startled. Then unexpectedly, the table began to move round and round on its own. We all had to stand up to try to keep hold of it.

This spirit's energy was strong.

I asked the spirit to move the table as a sign for 'Yes' and keep still for 'No'.

'Are you the soldier people keep seeing on the stairs?' Straight away a huge bang emitted from the table.

'OK. Can you show us where you are?'

The table shook and wobbled. Quickly in jerky movements, it walked itself to the top of the stairs, leading us all.

I was delighted, and not at all scared. Now I wanted to know why he had taken his own life. Through a series of questions, I and the rest of the team discovered that this young man had been injured during the war and had been brought here to recover. It was whilst he was recuperating that he had heard that his sweetheart had been killed during the Blitz. With his heart broken, he had taken a gun and shot himself.

The spirit of the young soldier was unable to let go of his distress, and because of this, he hadn't been able to cross over to the other side.

We needed to help him. And that's just what we did. Sending a spirit to the other side can be very emotional, and I always like to do this, if possible. Some of the spirits are too scared to go into the light, but after some gentle persuasion from our spirit guides, the young soldier did eventually leave for the afterlife.

Just to double check, I called out again to him. Everything had stopped. There was no movement from the table and the atmosphere in the corridor had changed. It felt lighter somehow. No more would this soldier have to keep going through his turmoil. He was at peace at long last.

With the Tapestry Corridor now cleared and blessed, it was time to split up my team of ghost hunters. I formed a party with my team members: John G. on sound, Jon D. on camera, a historian and another female investigator. We went into what is called the Bones Room. Why this strange name? Because the room was stacked and filled with boxes, bags, filing cabinets and cupboards all full of human bones! These ancient remains had been found during archaeological digs around the grounds of the ancient castle.

As we descended down some stone steps, we heard what sounded like something heavy being dragged across the floor. We stopped dead in our tracks and then a bloodcurdling scream rang around the room.

We were all very nervous but Jon D., the camera man, was particularly scared, and we had to encourage him to walk into the pitch-black room.

As we slowly pushed further into the darkness, we all heard very clearly the sound of a man groaning. Poor Jon D. was absolutely terrified.

Meanwhile, I had sent Karl off into the Armoury. This was another totally creepy room. Swords and axes lined the walls. Suits of armour stood tall. Karl was instantly drawn to a side table, as he thought he had heard a noise coming from it.

He called out, and again heard something being moved on the table. He zoomed his night-vision camera over to the table. There, sitting in the middle, was an old-fashioned military drum.

And to his horror he could clearly see that the drum was moving, sliding across the table all by itself. Luckily Karl caught the whole thing on camera and the footage is a great piece of evidence.

Back in the Bones Room, one of my investigators suddenly began to panic and claimed he'd seen a face on the back wall. A man's face, all emaciated and grey. It completely spooked us and we were all ready to run. Of course, it didn't help when the historian whispered, 'You do know we're standing in what is really a mass grave. These bones have all been dug up from their final resting place. Perhaps their spirits aren't very happy about it.'

I shivered, not from the cold, but from the situation I had found myself in. I could feel eyes upon us all and I knew that something else was about to happen.

I called out, almost dreading a response: 'Who's here with us? Do something to let us know you can hear and see us.' I squeezed my eyes shut tight and waited with the rest of the team to see what happened next . . .

Karl, meanwhile, was still in the Armoury. Suddenly, with no explanation, he began to feel very sick. He picked up his camera and ran quickly out of the dark space. Was this sickness an effect of the paranormal? It certainly ties in with what many visitors have reported in the past.

I and my team, on the other hand, weren't feeling sick – just terrified. I had called out, asking the spirit to communicate with us by doing something – and after a slight pause, a large object suddenly hit our huddled group. We all screamed and charged up the stairs.

We were disorientated and petrified, scrambling over each other to get out. What had hit us? At that moment we were all so frightened, we didn't care. All we wanted to do was get out of the Bones Room.

After a couple of minutes spent calming down, we flicked our torches on and went back. We began to scan the floor – hoping to find the stone or rock we thought had hit us. But the only thing we could find on the floor was a human bone! With that we decided to get out and take a much-needed break.

After a strong cup of tea, we all chatted about our experiences and Karl showed us the footage of the moving drum. I was beside myself with excitement. We had actually caught a large object moving on its own! I was pleased with our investigation and ready to go home. But not all the investigators shared my view and they wanted to experience the Bones Room for themselves.

The historian, Karl and Stuart decided to head back down there.

Would they experience more poltergeist activity? It wasn't long before the three brave souls did indeed witness something frightening. Again, they could hear deep growls and groans and then *BAM!* Something hit the historian's head. He leaned forward and shook his hair, and out fell . . . a human tooth.

Karl had been feeling sick for a while, but this was the final straw. He ran into the toilets and vomited.

That was enough for me and the rest of the *Most Haunted* team. We had managed to capture a lot of paranormal phenomena. But now we were all ready to go home.

? DID YOU KNOW? ?

Liverpool Street Station in London is built on top of an ancient burial ground.

During the Great Plague of 1665 many of its victims were laid to rest in the area. Thirty skeletons were discovered in 2015 under the station. So, it's no wonder that there have long been stories that the old building and its tunnels are haunted.

Many new housing estates are also built on top of burial sites and, because of this, the spirits that were once laid to rest are thought to feel angry at being disturbed. As a result, it is believed that they cause mayhem, panic and hauntings in the new houses. So, here's a question . . . what was your house built on top of?

WHITTINGTON CASTLE

LOCATION
OSWESTRY, SHROPSHIRE

DATE OF INVESTIGATION
2016

GHOSTS

THE CAVALIER SOLDIER

A LITTLE BOY

GHOSTLY FACES

THE CLOAKED MALE FIGURE

MA SYKES

AN EVIL ENTITY

PARANORMAL ACTIVITY

SOUNDS OF SCREAMING, WHISTLING AND SINGING

MARCHING FOOTSTEPS

LIGHT ANOMALIES

A CHILD'S SOBS, LAUGHTER AND CRIES

BLASTS OF ICY COLD AIR

FEELINGS OF SICKNESS AND DEPRESSION

Whittington Castle

Whittington Castle sits in the heart of a twelve-acre site, on the border between Wales and England. Today you can see the remains of a twelfth-century castle. This castle looks like something you would expect to see in a movie, complete with battling knights and elegant fair maidens. In terms of looks, this is one of my favourite castles. And with a history spanning centuries, this building has a lot to offer any keen ghost hunter or historian.

The castle was originally a stronghold, and was perfectly placed because it was surrounded by treacherous marshlands. Many battles between the Welsh and English raged in and around its walls over time.

The last assault on the castle was in 1643 during the English Civil War, when it was attacked by Oliver Cromwell's Parliamentarians. No restoration work was undertaken after this attack and the inner bailey has remained uninhabited ever since. The castle would have been a difficult building to seize, as it was defended by a moat. Without it, perhaps the castle would have been taken much earlier by Cromwell's men. But fast forward to 2006, because something extraordinary was pulled out of the bottom of the moat. Armour was discovered, dating back to the Civil War.

Like so many castles, over the centuries Whittington also served as a court room and prison for the local area.

THE HAUNTINGS

THE CAVALIER SOLDIER

The ghost of a Royalist Cavalier soldier has been seen on many occasions in and around the building by staff and visitors to the castle. Could this spirit be the owner of the armour that was found in the moat? And if he is, then does he still think the war is raging on? Is he still protecting his beloved castle for his king?

A LITTLE BOY

At one end of the library there is a well. It's covered over now with perspex. But this well was once an important water supply for the castle. The ghost of a little boy is often seen and heard in this area. He walks across the library and straight through a wall.

Many people think that this little boy, probably a servant, was drowned, possibly murdered, in the well. The little boy's ghost likes to play with unsuspecting guests and often people report hearing running and laughter, and experience poltergeist activity in the room. Notably, books seem to have a life all of their own in the library.

GHOSTLY FACES

Ghostly dark faces are often seen by locals, peering at them through the windows. Seconds later, they completely vanish.

THE CLOAKED MALE FIGURE

The castle has a huge main gateway and when only a couple of staff are present in the building, they report the sighting of a shadowy, cloaked figure. Who this ghost is no one knows, but he always makes his presence known in the same spot. Maybe he was once a guard and feels that the castle still needs protecting.

MA SYKES

A cottage within the grounds of the castle was once a laundry. During the First World War, Ma Sykes, as she was known, was in charge of cleaning and pressing the uniforms of soldiers stationed nearby. During the day, Ma worked relentlessly and at night she retired to her rooms upstairs. She would often sit in her rocking chair and fall asleep. After her death many witnesses have seen Ma Sykes rocking back and forth in her chair – but walking around her is what looks like a dark, menacing figure.

AN EVIL ENTITY

At the end of a bridge there is a tall brick building called the turret. Many fear to go into the lower part of this structure. People have often reported feeling unwell and claustrophobic in there. And sightings of shadowy figures have been seen in this building. I was looking forward to investigating in there!

THE INVESTIGATION

To begin this investigation, I was keen to get into the library. This was the place with the well where poltergeist activity had been reported. I hoped we would be able to catch this phenomenon on camera, so I took Karl in with me.

Karl was armed with a night-vision camera, and I held my torch like a weapon. I was a little scared. I often get frightened in places where poltergeist activity has been experienced, as I have frequently been the recipient of violent flying projectiles, from knives to crowbars. I wondered if I might get a book thrown at me.

In the pitch-dark library, many books lined the floor-to-ceiling shelves. On the ground in front of the shelves was the covered well. I stood on top of the perspex and began to call out. I closed my eyes as I spoke, willing the spirit of the little boy to come forward.

'Are there any children here? Can you hear me?' I whispered.

In an instant, both Karl and I heard loud footsteps walking above our heads.

We decided to dash upstairs to where we thought the noise had come from. But when we got there, breathless and excited, we saw no one, nor anything out of place.

Meanwhile, in a room that was once the Armoury, cameraman Stuart, sound recordist Darren and our demonologist had found the armour that had been discovered in the moat.

They decided between themselves that Darren should put on the armour and see if he could feel anything or see any images in his mind's eye. This is a technique called psychometry and many sensitive people and mediums use it as a way of communicating with spirits and looking into the past. They say that the item can hold energy from the person who used to own it. They close their eyes whilst touching the item and sometimes information comes through which can be verified by a historian or relative of the past owner.

Would Darren be able to sense anything?

Personally, I was keen to get into the court room. In my experience, there always seems to be a lot of paranormal activity in these places. Why? I believe that so much energy has been pushed out into the room over hundreds of years: anguish, terror and foreboding would have been felt by most of the castles' prisoners. This energy permeates the very fabric of a building and when the atmosphere is right, the ghosts come out to play.

In this court room, it's said that many people suddenly experience a dark feeling of depression and overwhelming sadness. Icy cold blasts of air assault the body without any warning. Hopefully, between Karl and myself, we could muster some positive energy that would entice the spirits to come out of the shadows and talk to us.

Standing in the centre of the room with a candle between us, I began to ask the spirits to join us. After what seemed like an age, we both heard loud footsteps marching quickly towards us and the whole floor shook. It was terrifying. We were both so taken by surprise that we stumbled backwards.

We took deep breaths and called out for the spirit to come towards us again. But this time nothing occurred. We waited again for a while and then I asked if the spirits could affect Darren or Stuart, who were over in the Armoury. Little did we know that that's exactly what would happen.

Darren was still wearing the armour and trying to see if he could sense anything. I have to say, when I saw this footage, I couldn't help but laugh as Darren *did* look a little strange in night vision, wearing a metal breastplate and a helmet. But my laughter soon faded as Darren started to sway from side to side.

'I don't feel good,' he said quietly to his companions.

'Come on, let's take it off before you fall over,' said Stuart, concerned. But as they began to take the armour off, Darren fainted.

Stuart managed to get the armour off Darren and, within seconds, poor Darren came to, feeling very sick. So, what had affected him? Perhaps the ghost of the Civil War soldier who once wore the armour didn't like Darren wearing it and had made him feel unwell. Or maybe he was just too hot in that suit and it made him faint?

After a tea break and a catch-up with each other, I decided to split the group up once more. This time I went back into the court room with Darren and although we didn't see or hear anything at the time, when we were editing the footage we captured, we saw a strange light anomaly. A peculiar-shaped bright light whizzed in a straight line above my head. What it was, we don't know. It moved too fast for an insect, that's for sure. Could it have been something paranormal? I believe so.

Karl and Stuart had been sent to the library. A locked-off night-vision camera was set up: a key component to capturing paranormal activity. We always like to position small night-vision cameras around empty haunted rooms, just in case we manage capture a ghost or a poltergeist at play.

After an initial look around, they heard footsteps walking above them again and so they sped quickly to the upper floor once more.

After they checked all was clear, they then heard thumping noises coming from the library.

They ran back downstairs and discovered lots of books covering the floor – which definitely hadn't been there before.

'That's the noise we must have heard from upstairs,' said Karl. 'I can't wait to see the locked-off camera footage. I bet we've got them falling off the shelves.'

When we met up again and looked at what the locked-off camera had caught, what we saw was astounding. There, right in the centre of the screen, one after the other, books were seemingly pushed off the shelf. *Bang . . . bang . . . bang!*

This certainly looked like poltergeist activity, and we had managed to capture it on camera.

I wondered who had moved the books. This activity did match what many other people had experienced. My guess is that the ghost of the little boy was responsible. I think he likes the idea of scaring people. Not in a bad way, just as a child's prank. Well, it definitely worked and I'm very grateful he decided to play with us that night.

Before we finished the investigation, we all gathered together for one last vigil. I thought it would be a good idea to conduct a séance in the former Armoury. I suggested that we all sit in a circle and place the breastplate in the centre of the floor.

As we called out for something to happen, for the soldier to communicate with us, the room grew very cold.

I told everyone to place their fingers on the breastplate, to see if we could get it to move in response to some questions. As we all leaned forward and asked various questions, the breastplate did in fact begin to vibrate. It was extraordinary. I asked the ghost of the soldier to move the piece of armour as a sign of 'Yes'. But suddenly Darren began to feel faint and sick again. He told us to carry on without him but sadly the vibrations on the armour began to fade and after a few minutes the activity died.

After a long but exciting night, I called a close to the investigation. We'd filmed some incredible poltergeist footage and had a really good time – well, apart from poor Darren, who only started to feel better as he walked out of the castle grounds.

DID YOU KNOW?

Anyone can try psychometry. If you fancy having a go yourself, here's how to do it:

Find a quiet space with no distracting noises where you won't be interrupted. Sit in a comfortable position, close your eyes and take calm, gentle breaths. Place your hands lightly on your lap with your palms facing upwards.

Ask a trusted companion to place an object in your hands. Keep your eyes closed! This object should be something precious to your companion that they have had in their possession for a long time.

Wait for feelings or images to come into your mind. Don't worry if nothing comes for a while. Sit patiently and wait.

Don't be afraid to speak out loud, no matter how strange the feelings and images are. They may not make sense to you, but your companion may well know what you are talking about.

If you do have success with your first try, that's great. If not, keep going. It took me a long time to get it and I'm really pleased I stuck with it.

Good luck!

OXFORD CASTLE

LOCATION
OXFORDSHIRE

DATE OF INVESTIGATION
2008

GHOSTS

THE MONK   *MARY BLANDY*

PRISON GUARDS   *A POLTERGEIST*

PARANORMAL ACTIVITY

WHITE MISTS   *OBJECTS THROWN AND MOVED*

MOANS AND GROANS   *LARGE DARK SHADOWS*

THE HISTORY

Oxford Castle

Oxford Castle was originally built under William the Conqueror's orders. A faithful and loyal subject of William was given the task of building a castle for his beloved king. Robert D'Oyly chose to construct the castle near a stream, which runs into the River Thames, as protection against invasion. The first stronghold was purely an earth mound with a wooden structure on top. But in 1073 that was replaced by stone fortifications and a keep.

Over time the castle was caught up in many battles and sieges but in 1230 Parliament decided that after so much conflict, and having been left to ruin, the castle was now unsuitable for military use and so was turned into a prison.

Prisons around that time in England were terrible places to be incarcerated. And Oxford was no exception. Brutal torture and barbaric practices and punishments were the order of the day. Some of these included tongue boring, whipping and branding.

During the Civil War, the Royalists made Oxford their capital, but Oliver Cromwell's army successfully besieged the city. In 1649, most of the stonework of the castle was replaced with earth bulwarks by the Parliamentarians who captured it.

After the Civil War, the castle became a prison again, where many executions were carried out – some by the notorious Jack Ketch. Ketch was an infamous public executioner during the seventeenth century, known for the barbaric and botched ways in which he put the condemned to death. Wielding an axe was his preferred way to do the dastardly deed and, in some cases, he performed the most hideous and painful of executions – hanging, drawing and quartering. Jack was so feared amongst the people that many referred to him as Satan.

The castle finally closed its doors as a prison in 1996 and has since reopened as a tourist attraction, hotel and restaurant.

I have, in fact, stayed in the hotel, and the rooms are old prison cells, but today all decked out with plush furnishings and a comfortable bed. Did I sleep through the night? Did I, heck!

THE HAUNTINGS

THE MONK

The ghost of a large monk, said to be very aggressive, has been heard shouting and swearing. This negative entity loves nothing better than to physically attack visitors and staff. Many believe that this ghost is responsible for the violent poltergeist activity that terrifies people in the dark crypt underneath the castle.

PRISON GUARDS

The crypt dates back over nine hundred years and has been witness to every single event in the castle's history. So, it's no surprise that, as well as the violent spirit of the monk, faceless ghostly guards are said to roam this area at night, presumably searching for prisoners to lock up.

Their shadows and footsteps are constantly heard in the dark, dank rooms down below.

Allegedly, during a night-time patrol of the castle, a security guard and his dog came across two black ghostly figures. Neither had arms or legs. The poor security dog barked and yelped as if in pain. The ghostly guards then dematerialised into thin air. The dog died a few days later. Its owner believed it died from shock and fear.

MARY BLANDY

Mary Blandy was executed at Oxford Prison on 6th April 1752, having been found guilty of poisoning her father using arsenic. Her father did not approve of her engagement to Captain William Cranstoun, because he'd discovered that Cranstoun was already married. Mary claimed that Cranstoun sent her a 'love potion' and told her to put it in her father's food to make him approve of their love match. After a thirteen-hour trial, thirty-two-year-old Mary was hanged. But until her final breath, she maintained her innocence and said that she was not aware that the potion was in fact arsenic.

Since her death her ghost has been witnessed many times, walking around the outside of the

castle and the area where she was hanged. Maybe her soul cannot rest as she believed she was tricked into poisoning her father.

A POLTERGEIST

A violent poltergeist resides in the crypt. This part of the castle is truly frightening. Stone walls and archways lead you into complete darkness. As you stand in the eerie blackness, a rush of cold air will squeeze your body and then the sounds of moans and groans can be heard permeating the area. Objects, such as stones and bits of wood, are thrown, sometimes with such violence that they have been known to hurt unsuspecting visitors. I believe, as do many others, that the ghostly monk is the one responsible for this cruel and frightening activity. Why? I hoped to find out.

THE INVESTIGATION

As soon as I stepped inside this magnificent structure, I knew we were in for an interesting and frightening night. I had goosebumps and felt as though many ghostly eyes were watching us.

We found a good base room; this is usually a room central to the haunted areas. It's best to use somewhere that isn't known to be haunted – so an investigator can feel safe and relaxed after a long vigil. This is also a place where monitors can be set up, showing images of the haunted areas. A bit like security cameras. Of course, I've been in base rooms, having a nice cup of tea, when knocking and tapping have suddenly begun and even a small fire has broken out in the room – so the base room cannot always be the safe haven you want it to be.

The camera crew set up locked-off night-vision cameras and positioned them in known haunted areas. Baseline readings were then measured and recorded. Once all this was done, we were ready to begin our investigation.

We kept all the lights on as we began to film. I wanted to start in the prison cells, as many people had seen dark shadows and heard ghostly moans and groans there. As we walked around the cold, stone rooms where prisoners were first brought into the castle, we heard and caught on camera the sounds of a man groaning. It was so loud and heartbreaking to hear. When we stopped talking and waited patiently for the next sound to be made, nothing happened. But when I began to talk, the moaning began once more. The ghost seemed to only want to make the terrible noises when *I* was talking. Maybe it hated my voice!

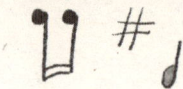

I decided to have a play with the spirit and sang three notes, asking if the ghost would copy me. Lo and behold, it actually repeated the three notes. Was this an entity wanting to play?

Still with the lights on, the team and I wandered down onto the bowels of the castle and settled in the ominous crypt. It really was a creepy place, and I didn't relish standing there in the darkness. But that's exactly what we had to do as ghost hunters. I asked the camera crew to turn all the lights off. It was now so dark I couldn't actually see my hand in front of my face and I felt terrified.

My fear was compounded when the same moan we had all heard earlier was picked up by the camera and sound equipment. It seemed really close, as if someone were standing next to us all.

With such great spiritual presence, I decided to start a séance. A large table was set up in the middle of the room. Five team members and I sat around the table whilst the cameraman and sound recordist stood nearby to hopefully capture the action.

I began by calling out for the monk, and, as soon as I did, the table began to shake – accompanied by a long frightening moan.

Everyone was on edge. The more questions we asked, the more the table began to move. Up and down. *Crash! Bang!* It almost had a life of its own, and the moaning and groaning was getting louder. It seemed we were communicating with the ghost of a very angry monk. But although the table continued to crash about, we weren't really getting any answers to our questions. So, I decided to use the Ouija board. Perhaps this monk could tell us more about himself using the letters on the board.

Within seconds of us all putting our fingers on the glass, it began to move quickly and with force.

'Why are you here?' asked a member of the team.

The glass quickly shot over to the letters *P*, then *O*, and finally *X*.

'What does that mean?' I asked my friends.

One of the team members was a historian and proceeded to ask the ghost various questions, with some great results.

'So, you caught a disease, the pox?'

The glass went over to the word, 'Yes'.

'And did it affect your skin, your face?'

Again, the glass shot over to the word, 'Yes'.

We were getting somewhere.

The historian continued: 'Were you thrown out of the monastery for having this disease?'

Well, that did it. The table went high in the air and then smashed back down. We all tried to keep our fingers on the glass, but it whizzed off the board and smashed to the ground.

Suddenly the room fell totally silent. I felt anxious. This spirit and the others who resided in the castle were strong, and I had a feeling they were about to let us know just how unhappy they were.

After a quick break, I sent Karl and cameramen, Ian and Geoff, up to the tower.

This was a tall structure. Spiral stone stairs wound their way up to the top, with rooms leading off at each level. It was very claustrophobic and allegedly very haunted. Although only sounds had been captured here, we hoped that the three men would experience something more.

As they made their way up to the top, Karl stopped suddenly and said he thought he could hear footsteps following them. They quickly continued their ascent but soon stopped as

Geoff cried out, 'Oh my God! That moan, did you hear it?'

'Yeah,' said Karl. 'It's like we've got someone below us and someone above us.'

'I don't like this at all,' said Geoff. 'I think I want to leave.'

They started to walk slowly back down the stairs, not wanting to go past where they had all just heard the deep groan coming from. Then the groan bellowed upwards at them.

The three men were now quaking in their boots as vocal assaults were hurled at them from the top and bottom of the stairs.

'Right, we've got all that on film,' said Karl. 'Let's make a run for it, and whatever happens, don't stop.'

And that's exactly what they did.

After hearing what had happened to Karl and

the others, I decided I wanted to experience this phenomenon for myself. So, I took cameraman Stuart and two other investigators with me.

We made it up the stone staircase and, disappointingly, heard nothing. I took us all into one of the rooms off the stairs and called out, hoping for a response.

'Hello, are there any spirits here with us? Are you watching us?'

Straight away we heard two loud bangs. Where the noises came from, we couldn't tell. Stuart then began to ask that the spirits show us a sign.

Again, within moments of Stuart asking, another enormous bang thundered through the room, causing us all to scream and cry out.

In my fear, I ran and stumbled backwards, hurting my ankle.

Stuart went to the door and found that it was now shut. He knew he had definitely left it open. Had a gust of wind blown the heavy wooden door shut? Upon closer inspection we discovered that the door wouldn't budge for us.

The large bang we had all heard, which had caused me to fall and hurt myself, must have been the sound of the door slamming shut. No living person could have done this because surely we would have heard them coming up the stairs. And we certainly never heard the huge metal bolt slide across.

The realisation suddenly struck home: something had locked us in!

Then I heard a deep growl reverberate around the dark room. We were trapped. And I knew we were not alone.

Stuart and I quickly got Karl on the phone and told him where we were and what had happened. I just hoped that in the time it took Karl to come up the stairs to the room, nothing else would happen to harm us. Whoever had locked us in was either a ghostly prankster or a malevolent spirit that wanted to scare and hurt us.

Well, they had certainly scared us.

We all waited with bated breath, too frightened to call out in case one of us was targeted.

Karl arrived quickly and captured on camera the massive bolt and demonstrated how it made a noise when being slid back.

As soon as we were let out, we all made a hasty retreat back down the stairs. But the ghosts hadn't given up yet. As we walked, the sounds of footsteps, growls, sighs and moans were captured on camera.

So, who had locked us in? Could it have been the angry monk? Or perhaps the spirit of Mary Blandy? I believe it could have been the ghosts of the prison guards, always on the lookout to capture and lock in new prisoners. Can you imagine if a lone investigator had gone to the castle and had been locked in? I wonder how long it would have been before someone let them out. When investigating haunted locations, always have your phone or a walkie-talkie handy. You just never know what might happen.

This investigation at Oxford Castle really did stick in my mind. The noises and poltergeist activity were magnificent and terrifying in equal measure. But being locked in a haunted tower is something I'll never forget and, because of that frightening experience, I always put a heavy object in front of an open door. Just in case.

DID YOU KNOW?

The spiral staircase has many spiritual meanings. In feng shui, the spiral staircase resembles chaos. In Yiddish this staircase is referred to as the 'shvindel trep' meaning 'swindling steps', because you never know how close you are to the top or the bottom, causing confusion and claustrophobia.

If you dream of a spiral staircase, it indicates that you are going through a very confusing time in your life. If you are in the middle, the beginning or the top, it makes no difference. This dream is a warning that hard and confusing times are ahead.

HEVER CASTLE

LOCATION

KENT

DATE OF INVESTIGATION

2007

GHOSTS

ANNE BOLEYN

HENRY VIII

A TALL MAN
RIDING A HORSE

PARANORMAL ACTIVITY

BEING TOUCHED BY UNSEEN
HANDS

DISTINCT ODOURS

A SENSE OF EVIL

VISITORS FEELING SICK

OBJECTS THROWN ACROSS
THE FLOOR

Hever Castle

This castle's original medieval construction began in 1383. It started life as a walled bailey and gatehouse and was built using stone quarried locally in Kent.

In the fifteenth and sixteenth centuries it became home to one of the most influential and ambitious families in the country: the Boleyns. This wealthy family added a large and comfortable Tudor dwelling within the defensive walls of the mighty castle.

A little girl was raised at the castle and her name was Anne Boleyn. She became the second wife of King Henry VIII and from this romance came events that changed the country forever. Because of her strong will and ambition, Anne refused to be the king's mistress and insisted the only way the king could have her was to marry her. But the king was already married and divorces were forbidden by the Roman Catholic Church. Henry split from the Catholic Church and made himself the head of the Church of England, so that he could divorce his first wife, Catherine of Aragon, and marry Anne.

After poor Anne failed to produce a male

heir, she was accused of adultery and treason, and executed.

Henry later gave Hever Castle to his fourth wife, Anne of Cleeves. When Anne of Cleeves died in 1557, the castle passed through many different families, each with their own stories of happiness and tragedy.

Sadly, like many historic buildings, the castle eventually fell into decline. But it just so happened that one of the world's richest men, William Waldorf Astor, bought the historic site in 1903. He spent much time, passion and money on restoring the castle. And because of him, Hever Castle still stands, proudly looking over a lake and beautiful gardens.

THE HAUNTINGS

ANNE BOLEYN

The ghost of Anne Boleyn is said to have been seen roaming the gardens on many occasions. Her spirit has also been spotted in one of the ground-floor rooms. A visitor is said to have seen the ghost of a young woman in her twenties, seemingly in distress, through a window from the outside. She looked to be beating her fists against the windowsill and scratching her fingers on the walls. The witness believed they had seen the ghost of Anne.

HENRY VIII

One of the largest bedrooms, complete with a four-poster bed, is said to have been where King Henry VIII slept. It's believed by some

that his ghost has been seen sitting in a chair in the corner of the room. People report a very large, grotesque-looking man just staring and watching.

Others believe this spirit is a disgruntled old man who doesn't like visitors in his home. Apparently, this apparition instils fear in all who witness it.

A TALL MAN RIDING A HORSE

In the Long Gallery, one of the most haunted locations within the castle, the ghost of a horse has been seen charging up and down the room. Upon its back sits a tall man. This is really odd, as the Long Gallery is two floors up!

THE INVESTIGATION

What an opportunity to investigate such a marvellous place! It was so exciting for me and my team to be able to spend the night in a castle that was once the home of Anne Boleyn, the mother of Queen Elizabeth I. Just to be able to walk around a building steeped in so much history was a thrill and a privilege. I hoped the ghosts would live up to their reputation.

After we had spent the day getting used to our surroundings, setting up all the equipment and making the necessary baseline tests, we began to get ready for the night's events.

I thought the Long Gallery would be a great place to start. So many people had had odd experiences here: from the ghostly galloping horse, to poltergeist activity, to feelings of sickness and unease. I wondered if we might hear the thunderous hooves of a charging horse or, better still, actually see its apparition. Imagine seeing the ghost of a horse, how wonderful and yet terrifying!

With all the lights off in the castle, we made our way up the creaking staircase and stopped at the top of the gallery. We all had to stand still because the floorboards were making so much noise.

We stood still in the pitch dark for a while and talked quietly between ourselves. We all agreed that we felt a little on edge.

After a while I began to call out, followed by other members of the team. Stuart was standing by a small staircase that went down to a small wooden door.

Suddenly he jumped and yelled out: 'I've just heard a woman's voice! She just said the word "Stella". Please tell me you all heard that?'

No one else had but we could tell from Stuart's reaction that he really thought he had heard something. I was annoyed, as I hadn't witnessed it and the sound man hadn't picked it up either.

We all moved down the small stairs and through the door where Stuart had heard the voice. It led into another dark chamber. Through our night-vision cameras we could see a metal door at the end of it.

Suddenly, Karl heard knocking. 'I think it's coming from that door,' he said, pointing and moving quickly to the door. He stood and placed an ear to it, and the rest of us all squeezed close. Sure enough, a knocking noise was coming from the other side. It wasn't the usual knocking and tapping that we hear on investigations when a spirit is trying to communicate with us. This was as if someone were really knocking at the door to come in.

One of the investigators slowly opened the door and discovered that no one was there. He said he'd stay on the other side and close it again, just to see if anything moved.

We all watched as he went into the other room. Suddenly the door began to knock again

as before. The investigator came back in and told us that he had heard the noise very clearly but did not see any of the furniture move. How extraordinary and wonderful.

When I asked who was with us, the answer was unclear, although when I asked how many spirits were with us, four loud deliberate bangs came from beneath the floor.

Off we all went to the minstrels' gallery next, which overlooked the Great Hall. A couple of us sat around a séance table and readied ourselves to begin. But we all froze as we heard the distinct sound of heavy footsteps creaking along the wooden floorboards. Then the creaking became louder as if someone were leaning against the wooden railings. It was almost as though someone had walked into the room to see what we were up to.

As I began to close my eyes and concentrate, the table started to vibrate. It felt like I had placed my fingers on top of a washing machine on a spin cycle. The table continued to rumble. The energies that were with us were close and I could tell they were eager to communicate.

My excitement soon evaporated though, when the vibrations faded into nothing. How

frustrating. But we were all uplifted as one investigator, who was using an infrared imaging camera, caught what looked like a set of footprints down below in the Great Hall.

They were directly below us and incredibly clear. What was really odd was that there were no footprints in front or behind. How had these two prints got there and who had made them? I was delighted, as was the rest of the team. We had caught something unexplainable on camera.

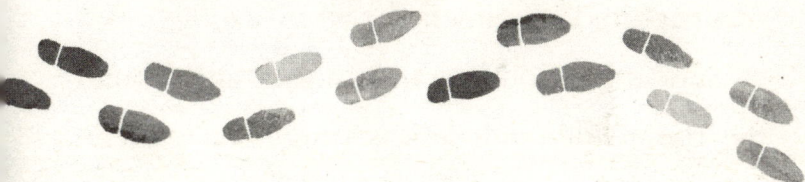

With renewed enthusiasm, I sent Karl and Stuart off to the Anne of Cleeves Room. As soon as they walked into the space, their nerves were off the scale. Why was this room having such an effect on them? It would soon become apparent.

Loud banging and knocking seemed to surround them. The noises soon turned to what seemed like pounding. It came from the walls, the floor, the ceiling.

'This is crazy,' whispered Karl, panning the night-vision camera around the room.

'I can't pinpoint where the noise is coming from,' said Stuart.

Both men were frozen to the spot. Their fear was captured on camera for all to see.

Suddenly a loud, strange noise rang around the room. Although it was caught on camera, even to this day, I've no idea what it was. I can only describe it as a long whine. It could have been what's called a death rattle, the last noise a human makes before they pass over.

The sound was truly terrible, and it felt evil to

Karl and Stuart. They decided they couldn't take any more and left in a hurry.

I, on the other hand, was sticking it out with two other investigators in Anne Boleyn's room. Although her ghost had been witnessed in other parts of the castle, I was hoping that she would make an appearance in her old quarters.

We had already heard moaning and crying and knew that we definitely had spiritual company. But who was with us? Could it be Anne? I was desperate to know. And so I began to ask questions, over and over again.

One of the investigators heard footsteps coming from the hallway and so we opened the door. I moved my camera to look down the corridor and instantly got a shock. There, to my right, was what I thought was the outline of a woman wearing a long, old-fashioned dress.

What time period she was from, I couldn't tell, but I definitely saw her. She was just staring.

'Oh my God!' I cried, and my camera began to shake. 'I could have sworn I just saw a woman looking at us.'

Sadly, when I looked at the footage, I couldn't make out the image I thought I saw. But I know I *did* see a ghostly woman and I'm hoping it was the spirit of Anne Boleyn.

Hever Castle, in my opinion, is definitely haunted and its spirits are aplenty. You only have to think of all the trauma that must have been witnessed, not just by Anne, but her family too, during those turbulent times. It's little wonder we heard and experienced so much paranormal activity there.

DID YOU KNOW?

Anne Boleyn's ghost has been seen in many different locations around the country. As well as Hever Castle, she has been witnessed at Windsor Castle and Hampton Court Palace. But the best sighting is this . . .

One dark night, at the Tower of London, the location where Anne was executed, a guard saw what he described as a woman resembling Anne. She appeared right in front of him, scaring him half to death. He was so terrified that he plunged his bayonet into her ghostly torso and then watched in horror as her image completely faded away.

So, if you visit any of the above locations, keep your eyes peeled for the ghost of the doomed queen, Anne Boleyn.

TAUNTON CASTLE

DATE OF INVESTIGATION

2006

LOCATION

SOMERSET

GHOSTS

THE JUDGE

THE GREY LADY

A YOUNG WOMAN

A YOUNG MAN NAMED LIONEL

A CAVALIER

PARANORMAL ACTIVITY

TEMPERATURE DROPS

POLTERGEIST ACTIVITY

FEELINGS OF BEING WATCHED

STRANGULATION

MALE AND FEMALE VOICES

FEELINGS OF UNEASE

THE HISTORY

Taunton Castle

Taunton Castle was originally built in 1129 by William Giffard, who was both the Lord Chancellor of King Henry I and the Bishop of Winchester. This structure was built for the bishops and the Church, and was an administrative centre and a status symbol.

Many people visited this impressive place, including King John and his son Henry III. The castle was altered during the medieval period and then again during Tudor times. But its most notorious claim to fame has to be the Monmouth Rebellion. In 1685 the Protestant James Scott, the Duke of Monmouth (who was the illegitimate son of King Charles II) raised an army to try to dethrone the Catholic King James II. With the uprising of peasant soldiers on his side, the Duke of Monmouth felt sure his rebellion would free his country from the wrongful king. Unfortunately, the rebellion didn't go well, and the duke's army was defeated at the Battle of Sedgemoor in 1685.

The Duke of Monmouth and many of his surviving men were captured. The duke was beheaded for treason and his soldiers were sent to Taunton Castle to be tried by the infamous Judge Jeffreys. Around 500 men were imprisoned in the castle and eventually tried for high treason before being brutally hanged, drawn and quartered.

It is said that at the crossroads of Somerset, every tree was stained with the blood of traitors left to hang and rot, or from their severed body parts. A warning to all from the king.

Now the castle is a museum and hotel that welcomes visitors from all over the world.

THE HAUNTINGS

THE JUDGE

In 1685, Judge George Jeffreys conducted the Bloody Assizes after the Duke of Monmouth's rebellion, in a room that is now a museum. He tried over 500 men, condemning more than 200 of them to death. His ghostly image is sometimes seen walking along the empty corridors of the castle.

I have come across this infamous spirit many times and I believe his ghost doesn't want to face what awaits him on the other side. Is he too scared to meet his maker? I would think so, after his severe, cruel and unfair trials.

THE GREY LADY

Seen closely following the judge's apparition is the ghostly sight of a woman dressed in grey seventeenth-century clothing. No one knows who this spirit could be and why she is seen at the same time as the judge.

A YOUNG WOMAN

The apparition of a young woman has been seen regularly all over the building. Some people say that she was made to watch her brother's execution.

Was he one of the many soldiers executed after the Monmouth Rebellion?

A YOUNG MAN NAMED LIONEL

The spirit of a young man has often been felt in the castle house. It's believed his name is Lionel and that during the early part of the twentieth century, he died under mysterious circumstances. A family did live in the castle house during this time but information regarding Lionel's demise has always been difficult to find.

A CAVALIER

In the castle house, the ghost of a Civil War Royalist soldier has been witnessed walking up and down the stairs. The castle was occupied by the Parliamentarians during the Civil War but besieged by the Royalist Cavaliers in 1645.

THE BURIAL GROUND

If you park your car in the castle's car park in the dark, keep your eyes peeled as the place is actually right on top of an Anglo-Saxon burial ground. Strange lights have been seen in and around that area of the castle.

THE MUSEUM

Inside the museum, a vast hall complete with a balcony overlooking the space below is the location where Judge Jeffreys gave out his terrifying sentences.

In this area, many staff members and visitors have had a feeling of unease and always felt that they were being looked upon by hidden eyes.

One poor curator was at the top of a ladder painting one of the walls when he suddenly felt a terrible chill. He became so cold and fearful, he climbed down and tried to regain his composure.

Another of the custodians was cleaning one of the glass cases. In one swift movement he felt someone grab him around the neck. He couldn't see any reflection in the glass. He described the sensation as if a rope had been placed around his neck and was being tightened.

A poltergeist is also thought to lurk in this area.

CASTLE HOUSE

This whole house is said to be riddled with paranormal activity, from the ghostly sightings of the Cavalier soldier and the phantom of the young, bereaved woman, to the bizarre sight of objects disappearing and appearing in different locations.

Some members of the staff refuse to come into the bedroom area as they feel frightened. They report it always feels oppressive and freezing cold.

THE INVESTIGATION

This castle has a bloody history; so many people have been imprisoned and tried here. The terror and fear must have been too much to bear at times. And I believe that's why so much paranormal activity is reported within it.

On the day of the investigation, the rest of my team and I waited patiently for the sun to set so we could get started. When the castle was plunged into total darkness, I gave the order to synchronise cameras and for us to begin.

I wanted to get into the main museum, the room where the Bloody Assizes had taken place all those hundreds of years ago. Would the ghost of Judge Jeffreys come out to play? I hoped so.

Cameraman Jon D. and I shone our torches around the vast room and tried to take in our peculiar surroundings. The room was full of glass cabinets, showing items from the castle and surrounding area, telling the story of the castle to the present day.

It was a really eerie and creepy place to be wandering about in. Before I'd become acquainted with the area, I jumped at my own reflection in one of the glass cases.

I began to call out to the ghosts, hoping one of them would make a noise, so we would know they were watching us.

'Come on, come and say hello. Are you here, Judge Jeffreys?' In response, a loud bang came

from upstairs, followed by a shuffling noise as if someone were moving about up there. Instantly, we made for the balcony, but upon reaching it discovered there was no one there.

I immediately felt uneasy in the place where the infamous judge would have sat, leaning forward, staring at prisoners with unkind eyes. Was he here, watching us now?

We shuffled back down the stairs and, as we reached the bottom, Jon and I both distinctly heard a long sigh. I do hate it when ghosts growl or sigh really close to my face. It makes me really jumpy.

It wasn't long before something gave me another fright and that was the sight of a black shadow flitting in between the cabinets. Jon whispered that he was starting to feel really nervous, so we decided to take a quick break.

Meanwhile, I had sent a cameraman, Ian, and another brave ghost hunter to the library. They were sitting quietly, just listening for footsteps or unusual noises. Ian's torch suddenly went out, plunging them both into total darkness.

'I put fresh batteries in that just before we started,' said Ian.

The other investigator asked out loud: 'Who's here with us? Have you made the light go out?'

A faint knocking spooked them both, but they carried on asking a series of questions, trying to find out who this ghost was. They were amazed to discover that it was someone from the Anglo-Saxon burial ground which the castle was originally built on.

But it wasn't long before their nerves got the better of them.

'Wow! Did you hear that?' cried Ian, sounding agitated.

'Yeah, it was a whisper.'

'Right in my ear,' said Ian, rubbing the side of his face.

I love watching this piece of footage because you can clearly hear a whisper and it doesn't come from the two investigators. Ian was just about to suggest that they move to another area, when he jumped up, convinced something had touched his head.

Karl and Stuart, meanwhile, had been instructed to go up to the attic. It was another place none of the castle workers wanted to visit. I suggested to them that they try some table tipping. This is where two or more people sit around a table and place their fingertips gently on the table's surface. They call out for the spirits to join them and ask them to vibrate the table or move it across the room. I love this type of communication, because when the activity begins, you never want it to stop.

Karl and Stuart began and were amazed to find that whoever was with them in that dark space was willing to play the game. Up and down that table went, much to the astonishment of the two investigators. In fact, it is the only footage of table tipping where all four legs come off the floor at once. It was incredible. But although the activity was caught on camera, the spirit responsible didn't want to reveal their identity.

After a break, I called all the investigators together and we headed up to the castle house bedroom. This is the room where the spirit of Lionel has been felt and witnessed. I hoped he would come and talk to us.

There were about eight of us in this small room. It was a hot summer's evening, so we were all feeling the heat. I felt tired, so sat down on the floor. It wasn't long before I began to feel a slight cold draught behind me. I panned my torch over to where I felt it coming from but there wasn't anything there that could have caused such a breeze.

One of the investigators holding the infrared camera informed me, though, that there was definitely a cold spot behind me. Everyone crowded round the camera and was amazed to see the cold spot clearly becoming bigger and bigger. I could really feel the icy cold, and it was getting too much, so I moved away.

I encouraged another investigator to stand in the position where the cold spot was while I looked at the infrared screen. I watched in wonder as the colour green began to spread all over the investigator.

'I'm freezing,' she said through gritted teeth.

I asked if this was Lionel but frustratingly, yet again, there was no response.

After the cold spot mysteriously dissipated, I suggested that we all go up to the attic. After all, this had been a great space for Karl and Stuart. Perhaps if all of us were together we would experience some more paranormal phenomena.

As soon as we got to the top of the stairs, I instantly felt dizzy, and I wasn't on my own. Everyone complained of feeling sick. In fact, one investigator compared it to sea sickness. Another felt like they were on a fairground ride.

'Who's here?' I asked, hoping to get a response. Something was affecting us all – that was for sure.

Suddenly, there was a loud thud and because it was so dark in the room, no one knew what had happened. It was only when we put our torches on that we saw both Karl and the sound man John G. had fainted.

Panicking, we went to their aid and managed to bring them round. Neither Karl nor John knew what had happened to them and both looked incredibly confused.

I knew that the investigation had to come to an end and so we packed up. Stuart helped Karl down the stairs and out of the castle, but halfway down the stairs, Karl fainted again and hit his head on the steps.

John was now completely awake, although he still complained of feeling sick and dizzy.

As we were leaving the building, we found someone or something had placed a chair to try to block our exit. There it sat, a large chair, right in the middle of the corridor. Was this a poltergeist at play? I suspected so. It certainly felt as though something malevolent was present and meant us harm. We made a hasty retreat.

My time at Taunton Castle was fascinating, although at times a little frustrating. I always love to try to find out who is haunting these buildings. Sometimes you get answers, other times you're just left with more questions.

I think that this castle has witnessed so much distress, it will never be able to rid itself of the terrible emotions and memories. That's why I believe this place will always be haunted.

DID YOU KNOW?

Another haunted location where Hanging Judge Jeffreys held his court was the Skirrid Mountain Inn in South Wales. It's said that more than 180 people were hanged in the inn from an old beam upstairs. Even now, you can see the mark where the rope was positioned.

I have investigated this small pub, and let me tell you, that was a night to remember. And I don't think the landlord will ever forget it either. That place was filled to the rafters with ghosts!

CORVIN CASTLE & HOUSKA CASTLE

DATE OF INVESTIGATIONS
2010

LOCATION
ROMANIA
CZECH REPUBLIC

GHOSTS
VLAD THE IMPALER

A MONK

DEMONIC CREATURES

THE DEVIL

PARANORMAL ACTIVITY
OBJECTS THROWN WITH FORCE

SMELLS

FOOTSTEPS

KNOCKING SOUNDS

GHOSTLY IMAGES

STRANGE LIGHTS

DEMONIC VOICES

HOUSKA CASTLE

CORVIN CASTLE

THE HISTORY

Corvin Castle

Houska Castle

Corvin, also known as Hunyadi Castle, was built in 1440 and is one of the largest castles in Europe. It was built by John Hunyadi, who was the governor of Transylvania at the time. As well as being a fortress, the impressive structure was also used as a prison. So, as you can imagine, this building has seen its fair share of death and despair.

Allegedly, Vlad Tepes, or to call him by his other name, Vlad the Impaler, was held in the dungeons here during his exile. It's said that while he was imprisoned, he became so enraged, it made his thirst for blood more engulfing. This man was to become a legend, not only for his torturous ways of impaling his enemies on spikes but also because hundreds of years later, Bram Stoker based his character, *Dracula*, on him.

The second castle we investigated was Houska Castle. A place steeped in history, black magic and terror. This location has such a ghastly reputation that the locals don't like to visit it. In its grounds lies a hole, a deep dark chasm which the villagers refer to as the Gate to Hell. The villagers believe that the castle was built directly on top of this gateway to Hell. Many people have tried to fill in the hole, but folklore says no one was ever able to fill it up to the top.

Instead, they built a chapel over the site. During the construction of the chapel, it is said that prisoners who had been condemned to death were given their chance for freedom if they agreed to be dropped down the hole. Once pulled back up, they could describe what they had experienced down in the Gate to Hell. Only then would they be set free. The first prisoner was dropped down on a seat and rope. Bloodcurdling screams could be heard coming from the dark depths below. When the poor unfortunate man was hauled back up, he had aged thirty years. He died two days later. What had he seen down there? Many people believe he had witnessed the Devil himself. In fact, after observing this poor man's demise, the other prisoners refused to enter the gateway to Hell and preferred to face execution.

During the Second World War, the Nazis occupied the castle and locals reported seeing strange lights coming from the building. Were the soldiers dabbling in the Dark Arts too?

It's also believed that the ghost of a monk dressed in black has been seen guarding the hole.

These two investigations were a once-in-a-lifetime experience. We had been given complete access to two massive European castles, and we were to broadcast our every move, scream and scare LIVE! And boy, there were plenty.

We went live across the nation over three nights and little did we know that when we finished the show something evil had followed us home . . .

THE HAUNTINGS

VLAD THE IMPALER

It's said that Vlad's ghost has been seen in the Knight's Hall and around the entrance to the dungeon at Corvin Castle. This entrance is in the floor of the hall. Many people have described seeing a large man wearing a tall hat.

A MONK

A black-robed monk has been witnessed in the Capistrano Tower at Corvin Castle. He was apparently caught spying on the noblemen and for his sins, he lost his life. Allegedly he was walled up, buried alive behind the bricks of the tower, and ever since then his phantom has been seen flitting around the place where his fate was sealed.

DEMONIC CREATURES

Horrendous and evil creatures are said to live inside the Gate to Hell at Houska Castle. One being a hybrid monster that is a cross between a human, a bulldog and a frog! I think if I saw that spectre, I wouldn't know whether to laugh or scream.

THE DEVIL

Many believe that the Devil himself resides within the Gate to Hell. What makes me think that there's some truth to this is the fact that the villagers were allegedly so scared by something horrific, they built the chapel over the top to stop any evil energy pouring out. Cement and stone were placed over the hole, but still to this day, locals keep their distance. To be that afraid of something makes you think, doesn't it? What was it they were trying to contain?

THE INVESTIGATIONS

CORVIN CASTLE

This final part of the book is very frightening, so if you're unsure whether you can handle it, I suggest you put the book down or speak to an adult first. Certainly don't read it by yourself after dark! What happened in these two investigations were some of the most terrifying experiences of my life.

The sheer size and impressive sight of Corvin Castle made my knees go weak when we arrived. It was so immense, and I and the rest of the team kept having to pinch ourselves that we were really there.

We were all terribly nervous, more so than usual. As always with live investigations, the biggest question was, would we capture any paranormal activity? The investigation is real and there is no fakery whatsoever, so the reality is if the ghosts don't want to communicate then you really feel that you are letting the audience down.

I remember saying a little prayer before we went on air, begging the ghosts to come out of the shadows and join us.

The prayer must have worked because every night we encountered so much, from poltergeist activity to Ouija board tables moving on their own!

During our first night in Corvin Castle I decided

to take the team into the Knight's Hall. Certain members of the team were terrified by this part of the castle and actually refused to come in to begin with. The locals had warned us to protect ourselves and my team members felt something very evil there.

Eventually, though, I managed to persuade all the *Most Haunted* team to join me. The hall was an enormous church-like space: cavernous and very foreboding. Everyone was on edge, especially as we had been told to protect ourselves.

In the middle of the stone floor was a trap door and I pulled it open. Inside was what looked to be the remains of dungeons. It was a hellish place where many poor souls had been kept until the decision was made about their fate.

As we were standing looking down into the pit of doom, Karl shouted out, falling backwards. 'There!' he said, pointing towards the brick wall and some wooden steps that went down into the pit. 'I've just seen a man. He was very tall and wearing a hat.'

I asked him for more details.

'He was big and tall and was wearing a funny hat, it looked like a marshmallow.'

I called out to our historian and after Karl described the ghost again, the historian confirmed that Vlad the Impaler matched Karl's description.

So now, as you can imagine, we were all very excited and keen to carry on. I decided that we must all go down into the dungeon and see what other ghosts lurked below. Squeezing through the tiny entrance, four eager but nervous ghost hunters descended fifty feet down into the darkness. We went by means of a wooden ladder that protruded out of the vacuous black pit. There was a rope to hold too, hanging along one side, which seemed to drop down into nowhere. We slowly and carefully made our way with our night-vision and infrared cameras.

When we reached the bottom, the stone walls pressed around us. It was narrow down there, and very claustrophobic. Wasting no time, I began to call out to the ghosts to see if I would get a response.

The ghosts responded within seconds and the knocking began. It was loud and repetitive. Something didn't feel right. It suddenly seemed as if something could swallow us whole and I instantly wanted to flee. But I tried to remain professional and carry on.

Without warning, an object of some kind came hurtling down from above, hitting one of the investigators hard on the hand. This was swiftly followed by another, this time landing on the floor.

We were horrified to discover that two bones had been hurled at us. What could this mean? And were they human? We didn't know. I called out again, but the knocking stopped just as suddenly as it had begun and nothing else fell from above.

HOUSKA CASTLE

On the last night of the live investigation, we went to Houska Castle, in the Czech Republic. According to legend this thirteenth-century castle has mystified and concerned the locals for many years. It was built for no obvious reason and once construction was finished, no one seemed to live there.

Evil winged, dark creatures have been seen flying out of it: demons, ghosts and even a headless horse. Demonic spirits are said to roam inside the hole known as the Gate to Hell, and around the castle. Many people believe that one of the past owners dabbled in black magic, which gave this portal to Hell a more powerful hold on the castle and its inhabitants.

So, what would be the best way to find out if this hole was really the Gate to Hell? Well, in my wisdom, I decided that a Ouija board session in the chapel above the hole would be a great way to see if we could capture any other-worldly phenomena. Would the Devil come and have a chat with us?

As soon as we all gathered round the table, the temperature in the room dropped quickly. I called out to the Devil himself and began to chant some ancient words in Hebrew. As I spoke, something began to copy me. It was really spooky and frightening. A male voice echoed around the stone room. Now I really wished I hadn't suggested this stupid idea.

'If you are here, Devil, do something

extraordinary.' My voice sounded confident but inside I was shaking like a jelly.

Straight away a pounding noise, like a heartbeat, began to reverberate around the room. We could hear demonic growling (which was picked up by our microphone) and heavy thumping started under our feet. It was coming from the hole!

'I don't like this,' mumbled one investigator. 'I don't like it at all.'

We carried on. No messages were spelled out on the board but the growling and thumping under our feet continued until eventually they slowly died away. Silence fell over the room, and everything suddenly stopped.

After the show and investigation had finished, we and all the tech crew began to pack away the cameras and other equipment. One technician was pulling a cable from inside the castle. Suddenly he felt himself being pushed forward and then to his horror he fell into a manhole. As he was being pulled back up, he alerted the team that he thought he had broken his ankle. Immediately our paramedics were called to help, but mysteriously they seemed to have disappeared from the site. After a telephone call to them, they told us that a man in an old-fashioned costume had told them to leave.

We didn't have anyone wearing a costume on the team. So, who was this mysterious man and where had he gone?

When we had all arrived back home in England, I was shocked when one after the other, my fellow ghost hunters began to call me to tell me of terrible things that had happened to them on the day of their return.

One investigator reported that her fifty-year-old father had wanted to go to the pub. The pub was situated at the top of a steep hill. He said, 'One of these days that hill is going to kill me.' He made it up the hill and into the pub. He took one gulp of his favourite beer and then fell on the floor and died.

Another investigator reported that his beloved dog had just keeled over in the garden, dead from heart failure.

One of the cameramen came home to find that his business had crumbled, and he'd lost all of his money.

Another investigator reported that a random car had smashed straight into the front of his house. Fortunately, no one was injured.

And then I had my own brush with danger. I decided to go for a ride on my horse. We were going down a country lane and suddenly, with no explanation, the usually very placid horse reared high in the air and fell backwards. It was as if something had stood in front of it and scared it. Fortunately, I threw myself off just in time as the horse landed on its back. If I hadn't been quick, I know I would have died. The horse wasn't injured and got up and shook itself. I didn't get back on. I walked, leading the horse back home.

What was happening here? We were all frightened and I just knew in my heart and gut that something bad had followed us home from abroad. And I suspected it had something to do with the Gate to Hell. We needed help! So the only thing I could think of was to speak to someone from the Church. I was in no doubt that we needed a blessing.

I phoned the vicar and briefly explained to him where we had been and what had been happening to us all. I was a bit embarrassed because it's not every day that you tell someone you've been to Transylvania and spent time in two haunted castles on the lookout for Dracula and the Devil!

The vicar couldn't have been more understanding and believed everything we told him. As soon as we could all get together, we arrived at the church and went straight to the font, where he blessed us with holy water.

I remember feeling the water slide down my face and crying, I was so overcome with emotion. The vicar hugged me and said that everything would be fine from now on as long as I didn't try to contact spirits ever again. I felt terrible as I bit my lip and said, 'I can't promise that, but I'll try.'

None of us will forget our time in Corvin and Houska Castles. We know that there were definitely energies and powers there that cannot be explained. I think that all the torture and imprisonment that occurred within the walls had soaked into the atmosphere and tainted the very fabric of both buildings. I believe these castles are most certainly haunted, but possibly not just by poltergeists and the ghosts of monks and Vlad the Impaler – but by something even more sinister.

Karl was convinced that he had seen the ghost of Vlad the Impaler at Corvin Castle and I and the rest of the team had seemingly unleashed something sitting over the Gate to Hell.

Would I go back and spend the night there? The answer to the vicar: 'Absolutely no way!' To my fellow ghost hunters: 'When do we leave?'

? DID YOU KNOW? ?

A sweet little town called Hellam in York County, Pennsylvania, USA, allegedly houses the seven gates to Hell!

According to urban myth and folklore passed down through generations, an old mental asylum that mistreated and murdered its patients turned into an evil abode, where seven entrances to Hell appeared. Seven gates were allegedly put up by an eccentric doctor, and so the legend goes, if you pass through all of them, you will go straight to Hell. Fancy coming with me to check it out?